Lili Boulanger

Deux Morceaux
pour
Violon et Piano

1. Nocturne
2. Cortège

ISBN 978-0-7935-3773-0

G. SCHIRMER, Inc.

DISTRIBUTED BY

HAL•LEONARD®
CORPORATION
7777 W. BLUEMOUND RD. P.O. BOX 13819 MILWAUKEE, WI 53213

ED. 3273

Lili Boulanger

(August 21, 1893 - March 15, 1918)

Composer Henry Barraud wrote: "The oeuvre of Lili Boulanger is a monument realized. It is not simply the promise of great work to come, but the achievement of an exquisite body of work by a composer of accomplished style, firmly rooted in a classicism which owes nothing to a School but solely to the natural perception which stems from a penetrating intelligence and talent."

At the age of sixteen Lili Boulanger knew that she would be a composer. Although her delicate health prevented her from attending school regularly or from going to concerts, she studied with her sister, Nadia Boulanger, and with Paul Vidal and Georges Caussade. As a child of six she showed extraordinary precocity, being able to sing Fauré songs, and she rapidly progressed in acquiring the skills of her destined profession. A member of the distinguished Boulanger family, whose grandfather, father and sister were appointed professors at the Conservatoire National in Paris, Lili Boulanger upheld the family tradition by becoming, as did her father and sister, a laureate of the Prix de Rome. In 1913, at age 20, she wrote the cantata *Faust et Hélène* for the Prix de Rome competition. The jury was hardly disposed to give the Prix to a young woman (a few years before it had refused her sister Nadia the first prize, reluctantly awarding her second prize) but *Faust et Hélène,* after only one-third of the work had been performed, was unanimously declared winner of the Grand Prix. The following day, at a public performance of the Concerts Colonne, the work received a triumphant reception.

Because of the outbreak of World War I, Lili Boulanger remained in Rome only one year, after which she gave without reserve of her already depleted energies to the *Comité Franco-Américain* to help families of musicians who had been called into military service. In 1916 she returned to Rome briefly but illness forced her to undergo a serious operation, after which her imminent death was foreseen. With complete serenity and faith she worked ceaselessly until her last hours on March 15, 1918. *Pie Jésu,* for Voice, Harp, Organ and String Quartet, her final work, conveys a unique and overwhelming fervor in its very simplicity: it was dictated note by note to her sister.

Although Lili Boulanger's early death undoubtedly deprived the world of a larger musical legacy, the oeuvre left by her is both significant and of considerable dimensions, numbering over fifty works which reflect a very personal and striking musical signature.

—Mario di Bonaventura

DUEX MORCEAUX
pour Violon et Piano

à ma chère Marie Danielle Parenteau

NOCTURNE

Lili Boulanger
(1893 - 1918)

* ou Flûte.

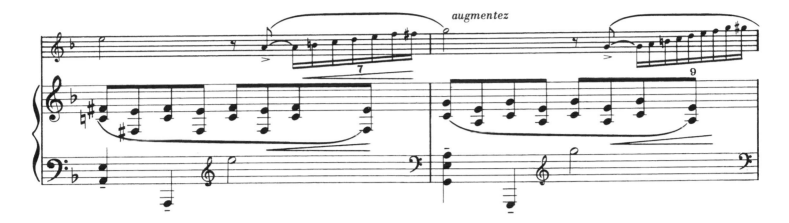

en dehors, doucement chanté

mettez la sourdine

très doux

cedez

un peu en dehors

cedez

en s'éloignant

III₂

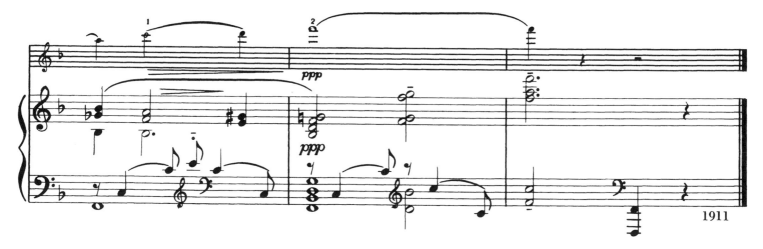

ppp

ppp

1911

DUEX MORCEAUX
pour Violon et Piano
à ma chère Marie Danielle Parenteau

NOCTURNE

Lili Boulanger

Violon*

* ou Flute.

* or Flute.

à Yvonne Astruc

CORTÈGE

Lili Boulanger

* *Faites légèrement attendre le 1ᵉʳ temps*

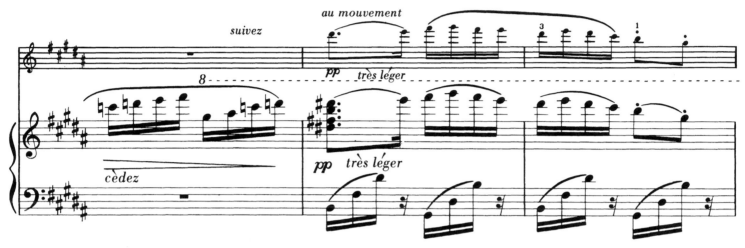

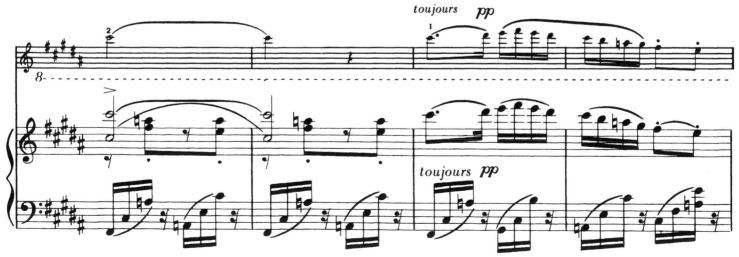

1914